by Murray Ogilvie

Lang**Syne**

PUBLISHING

WRITING *to* REMEMBER

Lang**Syne**

PUBLISHING

WRITING *to* REMEMBER

Strathclyde Business Centre
120 Carstairs Street, Glasgow G40 4JD
Tel: 0141 554 9944 Fax: 0141 554 9955
E-mail: info@scottish-memories.co.uk
www.langsyneshop.co.uk

Design by Dorothy Meikle
Printed by Hay Nisbet Press, Glasgow
© Lang Syne Publishers Ltd 2008

ISBN 1-85217-284-3
ISBN 978-1-85217-284-8

Borthwick

SEPTS NAMES:

Barthwick
Bortheik
Borthwyke
Borthwik
Borthwick
Borthweke
Borthuyke
Borthock
Borthek
Boirthvik
Boirthuik
Bowick
Borthick

Borthwick

MOTTO:
Qui conducit
("He Who Leads")

CREST:
A moor's head couped Proper
wreathed Argent and Sable.

TERRITORY:
The Scottish Borders.

Chapter one:

The origins of the clan system

by Rennie McOwan

The original Scottish clans of the Highlands and the great families of the Lowlands and Borders were gatherings of families, relatives, allies and neighbours for mutual protection against rivals or invaders.

Scotland experienced invasion from the Vikings, the Romans and English armies from the south. The Norman invasion of what is now England also had an influence on land-holding in Scotland. Some of these invaders stayed on and in time became 'Scottish'.

The word clan derives from the Gaelic language term 'clann', meaning children, and it was first used many centuries ago as communities were formed around tribal lands in glens and mountain fastnesses.

The format of clans changed over the centuries, but at its best the chief and his family held the land on behalf of all, like trustees, and the ordinary clansmen and women believed they had a blood relationship with the founder of their clan.

There were two way duties and obligations. An inadequate chief could be deposed and replaced by someone of greater ability.

Clan people had an immense pride in race. Their relationship with the chief was like adult children to a father and they had a real dignity.

The concept of clanship is very old and a more feudal notion of authority gradually crept in.

Pictland, for instance, was divided into seven principalities ruled by feudal leaders who were the strongest and most charismatic leaders of their particular groups.

By the sixth century the 'British' kingdoms of Strathclyde, Lothian and Celtic Dalriada (Argyll) had emerged and Scotland, as one nation, began to take shape in the time of King Kenneth MacAlpin.

Some chiefs claimed descent from

ancient kings which may not have been accurate in every case.

By the twelfth and thirteenth centuries the clans and families were more strongly brought under the central control of Scottish monarchs.

Lands were awarded and administered more and more under royal favour, yet the power of the area clan chiefs was still very great.

The long wars to ensure Scotland's independence against the expansionist ideas of English monarchs extended the influence of some clans and reduced the lands of others.

Those who supported Scotland's greatest king, Robert the Bruce, were awarded the territories of the families who had opposed his claim to the Scottish throne.

In the Scottish Borders country - the notorious Debatable Lands - the great families built up a ferocious reputation for providing warlike men accustomed to raiding into England and occasionally fighting one another.

Chiefs had the power to dispense justice

and to confiscate lands and clan warfare produced a society where martial virtues - courage,
hardiness, tenacity - were greatly admired.

Gradually the relationship between the
clans and the Crown became strained as Scottish
monarchs became more orientated to life in the
Lowlands and, on occasion, towards England.

The Highland clans spoke a different language, Gaelic, whereas the language of Lowland
Scotland and the court was Scots and in more
modern times, English.

Highlanders dressed differently, had different customs, and their wild mountain land
sometimes seemed almost foreign to people living in the Lowlands.

It must be emphasised that Gaelic culture
was very rich and story-telling, poetry, piping, the
clarsach (harp) and other music all flourished and
were greatly respected.

Highland culture was different from
other parts of Scotland but it was not inferior or
less sophisticated.

Central Government, whether in London

"The spirit of the clan means much to thousands of people"

or Edinburgh, sometimes saw the Gaelic clans as a challenge to their authority and some sent expeditions into the Highlands and west to crush the power of the Lords of the Isles.

Nevertheless, when the eighteenth century Jacobite Risings came along the cause of the Stuarts was mainly supported by Highland clans.

The word Jacobite comes from the Latin for James - Jacobus. The Jacobites wanted to restore the exiled Stuarts to the throne of Britain.

The monarchies of Scotland and England became one in 1603 when King James VI of Scotland (1st of England) gained the English throne after Queen Elizabeth died.

The Union of Parliaments of Scotland and England, the Treaty of Union, took place in 1707.

Some Highland clans, of course, and Lowland families opposed the Jacobites and supported the incoming Hanoverians.

After the Jacobite cause finally went down at Culloden in 1746 a kind of ethnic cleansing took place. The power of the chiefs was curtailed. Tartan and the pipes were banned in law.

Many emigrated, some because they wanted to, some because they were evicted by force. In addition, many Highlanders left for the cities of the south to seek work.

Many of the clan lands became home to sheep and deer shooting estates.

But the warlike traditions of the clans and the great Lowland and Border families lived on, with their descendants fighting bravely for freedom in two world wars.

Remember the men from whence you came, says the Gaelic proverb, and to that could be added the role of many heroic women.

The spirit of the clan, of having roots, whether Highland or Lowland, means much to thousands of people.

Chapter two:

The battling Borthwicks

Mystery surrounds the origin of the Borthwick clan. The most common belief is that they assumed their name from the Borthwick Water which lies between Selkirk and Roxburgh in the Scottish Borders. The family is said to descend from a Hungarian by the name of Andreas who arrived in Scotland with the court of Edgar Aetheling and his sister Margaret.

In 1066 William of Normandy conquered England and Edgar Aetheling, who should have succeeded to the English crown but was too young, went into exile in Scotland with his mother and sisters. They had previously been living in Hungary, indeed Edgar's mother was Hungarian, and were regally entertained by King Malcolm Canmore at his royal palace in Dunfermline. One of Edgar's sisters, Margaret, attracted Malcolm's eye and before long the couple were married. Andreas, as part of the royal retinue, was granted

land in the south of Scotland and from there his
family grew to become one of the foremost clans
in the country.

Over the years Borthwicks were involved
in several of the most talked about episodes in
Scottish history.

When Robert the Bruce was on his death-
bed in 1329 he asked that his heart be taken to the
Holy Land and carried into battle against the
"Infidels" because he had never gone on a
Crusade. Sir James Douglas volunteered to carry
out the king's final wish. Bruce's body was buried
in Dunfermline Abbey but his heart was placed in
a casket. In 1330 Sir James, accompanied by other
Scottish nobles, including Sir William Borthwick,
set off on a mini crusade from Berwick. At that
time the Moors occupied southern Spain and the
Spanish King Alfonso pleaded for help from foreign knights in his war against Muhammed IV,
Sultan of Granada. The Scots thought it would be
a great idea to join the Christian army in the battle to rid Europe of the infidels and headed for
Seville, where they arrived at the end of July. On

August 25 the Battle of Teba began. Douglas led
the advance and was soon involved in heavy
fighting. At one point the Saracens, under intense
pressure, were forced to flee and in the heat of the
battle Douglas chased after them until he found
himself almost alone. As he turned to rejoin the
main force he saw Sir William St Clair surround-
ed by Moors. Rather than escape, Douglas went to
his friend's rescue accompanied by a small number of Scots knights. But they were soon over-
whelmed. Douglas took the silver casket which
housed Robert The Bruce's heart, which he'd
been wearing round his neck, and threw it towards
the Moors shouting, "Now pass thou onward
before us, as thou wast wont, and I will follow
thee or die". Douglas and the knights who sur-
rounded him were all killed. King Alfonso's men
eventually overpowered their enemy and in the
final battle Sir William Borthwick personally
beheaded the leader of the Moor forces who
ambushed Douglas. To this day a Moor's head sits
in the Clan Borthwick crest. Sir William St Clair
was among the knights who died alongside

Douglas. The St Clairs and Borthwicks remained close through the centuries. When, in 1446, another Sir William St Clair built the sumptuous Rosslyn Chapel, the home of the Knights Templars who featured in the film *The Da Vinci Code*, the first Lord Borthwick was his cupbearer. This was a position of great trust and responsibility. Lord Borthwick's job was to serve the wine at St Clair's table. At that time Rosslyn was famed for its luxurious and often extravagant lifestyle. The cupbearer also had to swallow some of the wine before serving it, just to ensure it wasn't poisoned!

Sir William Borthwick it was who was created first Lord Borthwick and he was one of the Scottish noblemen who became substitute hostages for King James I of Scotland In 1398 King Robert III's health had deteriorated so much that the Scottish Parliament appointed his oldest son, David the Duke of Rothesay, to rule in his place. David had two very powerful uncles, both brothers to his father. One, Robert Stewart, the Duke of Albany, had his eye on the throne and in 1402 led a coup against David. He was helped by the Earl of

Douglas and the pair imprisoned David in Falkland Palace. Two months later David was found dead. Albany stated that the death was "by divine providence and not otherwise". But it later emerged that the 24-year-old captive had starved to death on his uncle's orders. King Robert had a younger son, James, who was born in 1394. Robert tried to protect him from Albany by sending him into hiding abroad. First James holed up at Dirleton Castle, East Lothian then on the Bass Rock on the coast just off North Berwick. From there he hoped to make his way to France. A merchant ship agreed to take him to the continent but it was boarded by pirates off Flamborough Head and James was seized and handed over to Henry IV of England. Exactly two weeks later, on April 4, 1406 Robert III died, heartbroken at the fate that had befallen his sons, and James I at the tender age of 12 was crowned king of Scotland. There was only one problem for James, he was a prisoner, although in some luxury, at Windsor Castle. The Scottish Parliament, meanwhile, appointed his uncle Robert, the Duke of Albany, as Governor of

Scotland. James was to spend 18 years in captivity. Then in 1423 the Treaty of London was signed. It provided for the release of James I in return for a ransom of £40,000 and the provision of 21 hostages as security until the money was paid. Under the terms of the treaty James had six years to pay in full and the hostages, all noblemen and including Lord Borthwick had to wait the full term before being set free. On his return to Scotland in around 1430 Lord Borthwick built a castle just outside Edinburgh so well it is still in existence today. It's not surprising it has lasted so long. The walls at the castle's base are thirteen feet thick, narrowing to six feet at the top and the structure was 110 feet high.

In 1511 the French were under attack from the Holy League, a military alliance which included the Papal States, Spain, the Holy Roman Empire and England among others. They approached King James IV of Scotland in the hope of resurrecting the Auld Alliance. In return for supporting his crusades to the Holy Land and his claim on the English throne, he agreed. In September 1513 Scottish forces marched into England from Edinburgh and, having disposed of resistance just south of the border, encamped on Flodden Hill. Despite positional and numerical advantage the Scots, missing their most able gunners who had been despatched to the aid of the French, were annihilated. James and his son Alexander, who was the Bishop of St Andrews, died along with two abbots, 11 earls, 15 lords and at least 10,000 others. Among them was William, the fourth Lord Borthwick who fought alongside his king. Another Borthwick played a prominent role in the battle. Robert Borthwick was the Scottish king's master gunner and had been responsible for designing and manufacturing seven huge canons, known as "The Seven Sisters". They were originally positioned in Edinburgh Castle but were moved by James to Flodden, where even their presence was not enough to save the Scots. The fifth Lord Borthwick, also William, was rewarded for his father's loyalty. He was given command of Stirling Castle and was made responsible for the safety of the infant king James V who was born just a year before Flodden.

Chapter three:

Loyal and true

The Borthwick's loyalty to the Scottish monarchy continued during the turbulent rule of James V and after his death when his daughter, Mary, Queen of Scots, became heir to the throne in the mid sixteenth century. She had been crowned not long after her birth in 1542.

Her mother, Mary of Guise, was a French aristocrat and she wanted her daughter to enjoy the same benefits she'd received from a strict Roman Catholic upbringing. At that time, though, a tide of Protestanism was sweeping through Scotland, led by John Knox. Lord John Borthwick was a powerful land owner. He was not in favour of the Reformation and openly supported Mary of Guise. Despite those strong, but unpopular, religious sympathies he found himself excommunicated. He had dared criticise the church and was found guilty of contempt of the Ecclesiastical Court of the See of St Andrews. William

Langlands, an officer of the court, was sent to
Borthwick Castle to deliver the letter of excom-
munication. However, he was intercepted by the
Lord's friends and thrown in the mill dam south of
the castle. Once he had dried he was made to eat
the letters, which had by now been soaked in
wine. The unfortunate Langlands was sent back to
St Andrews with a warning that any future
attempts to excommunicate his Lordship would
be met in the same way.

In 1548, in line with her mother's wishes,
Mary, Queen of Scots was sent to France where at
the age of 16 she married the Dauphin Francis
who was heir to the French crown. On his death
two years later in 1560 she returned to Scotland to
take the throne. Mary ensured her popularity by
doing little publicly to hinder the pace of the reformation, while celebrating mass in private. But
she made her first big mistake in 1565 when she
married her cousin Lord Darnley. He was younger
than her and immature for a 19-year-old. He was
unpopular with the other nobles and had a mean
and violent streak. Within a short time, Mary

became pregnant, but Darnley became jealous of Mary's private secretary, David Rizzio, and murdered him. Following the birth of their son, the future James VI of Scotland, Darnley continued to offend almost everyone who crossed his path. In February 1567 he died mysteriously after an explosion at a house in Edinburgh where he'd been staying. James Hepburn, fourth Earl of Bothwell and his supporters, were suspected of carrying out the killing. Mary herself was implicated, like she had been after the murder of Rizzio. Mary later married Bothwell, who had abducted her and imprisoned her for a week. There were rumours that he had raped her, thus forcing her to marry him. All of these events led to a public outcry and the Scottish nobility responded by challenging her right to rule. Matters came to a head in June 1567. At that time, one of Mary's closest friends and confidants was William, sixth Lord Borthwick. On June 7 Mary and Bothwell fled to Borthwick Castle, where they spent what was to be their last night together. Their host tried to protect the fugitives but forces led by the Earl of Morton and Lord Home tracked them down. While negotiations took place Mary slipped out of the castle under the cover of darkness disguised as a page boy. She eventually made her way to England where she was imprisoned and executed in 1587. Borthwick Castle, just outside Edinburgh near Gorebride, has been turned into a luxury hotel. Visitors can spend the night in the same room shared by Mary and Bothwell all those years ago.

The ninth Lord Borthwick, John, maintained the family's adherence to the royalist cause. During the third English Civil War the Scots declared their loyalty to King Charles II of England, who had been proclaimed King in Scotland in 1649. About 18 months later, in September 1650, The English parliamentary army, commanded by Oliver Cromwell defeated the Scots at the Battle of Dunbar. Cromwell then headed north and laid seige to Borthwick Castle. Lord John Borthwick held out for several days but was eventually forced to surrender. He negotiated favourable terms which allowed him and his family to leave unmolested and provided them with fifteen days to return and remove their belongings. He had previously married Lady Elizabeth Kerr, daughter of the Earl of Lothian but died in 1672 without an heir.

For the next 90 years the title was officially dormant. In 1727, however, Henry Borthwick made a claim to become the new Lord Borthwick. He was a direct descendant of Alexander Borthwick, who was the second son of the third Lord Borthwick. It wasn't until 1762 that the House of Lords ratified his claim and Henry became the tenth Lord Borthwick. Ten years later he, too, died without heir and once again the title became dormant. It stayed that way for over 200 years, despite many claims and counter-claims by members of the Borthwick clan. Finally, in 1986 Major John Henry Stuart Borthwick was recognised by the Lord Lyon as Borthwick of that Ilk, or chief of the clan. He also became the 23rd Lord Borthwick. On his death in 1996 he was succeeded by his son, John Hugh Borthwick.

Chapter four:

Hold the front page!

In more recent times many Borthwicks haved made names for themselves. However, none became quite as notorious as Martha "Mamah" Borthwick.

She was born in Boone, Iowa in June 1869. By the age of 23 she had graduated with a BA from the University of Michigan and later worked as a librarian. In 1899, she married Edwin Cheney, an electrical engineer from Illinois and they had two children, John and Martha. Mamah became friendly with Catherine, the wife of the world-famous American architect Frank Lloyd Wright. In 1903 Edwin Cheney commissioned Wright to design them a home. It's believed that Mamah and Frank Lloyd Wright began having an affair two years later. Mamah Cheney was a modern woman with interests outside the home. She was an early feminist and Wright viewed her as his intellectual equal. The two fell in love, even though Wright had been married for almost 20 years. Often the two could be seen taking rides in Wright's automobile through Oak Park, and they became the talk of the town. Wright's wife, Kitty, sure that this attachment would fade as others had, refused to grant him a divorce. Neither would Edwin Cheney grant one to Mamah. In 1909 the pair left their respective families and travelled to Europe, settling in Italy for about a year. When they got back to the USA they set up home at Taliesin in Spring Green, Wisconsin. Most of their friends were scandalised by their behaviour, a view expressed in the local paper. Due to Wright's fame the story reached the big papers in Chicago and they wrote critical articles predicting Wright would be arrested for immoral activities, even though the sheriff in Spring Green refused to press charges due to lack of evidence. The scandal affected Wright's career and the number of his commissions halved. He didn't get his next big project until 1916. But by then Mamah was dead, murdered in an act of violence which shocked America. On August 15, 1914, one of Wright's recently hired domestic workers murdered Mamah, both her children, three of Wright's associates, and a son of one of the associates. He was involved in a dispute with Wright and set fire to one wing of Taliesin, and attacked the seven people with an axe as they tried to escape the fire.

While one Borthwick was making the headlines, another two were writing them. Peter Borthwick was born in the Parish of Borthwick, Midlothian in 1804. He was educated at Edinburgh University and then went to Cambridge where he rapidly established a reputation as a brilliant public speaker. He'd gone to Cambridge with the intention of entering the English Church and had produced several learned works on theological subjects. But he was asked to consider a political career and succumbed to the lure of Westminster. This led, in 1834, to him being voted as Conservative MP for Evesham, Worcestershire. In 1847 he decided not to apply for re-election and instead to pursue a lucrative career as a barrister. However, before he could step in that direction he was asked to become the

Editor of *The Morning Post*, a London-based daily newspaper which had been published since 1772. A few years later his health began to deteriorate and he died in 1852, aged just 48. He was succeeded as Editor by his son Algernon, who had begun his journalistic career as the paper's Paris correspondent. In 1876 Algernon bought the paper and it began to focus on foreign affairs, literature and the arts. In another respect it was way ahead of its time – it began highlighting the lifestyles of the powerful and wealthy in the same way much of today's media is obssessed with the cult of celebrity. In 1885 Algernon followed his father's footsteps into Parliament by becoming the Conservative MP for Kensington South. In The House of Commons he was an ally of Lord Randolph Churchill, the father of war-time hero Sir Winston. In 1890 Algernon was knighted and five years later he became Baron Glenesk, a title which passed when he died in 1908. Sir Algernon's son Oliver became the paper's editor but died in his early 30s. When Sir Algernon died three years later control of *The Morning Post* passed to his daughter Lillias, who was married to Seymoor Henry Bathurst, the seventh Earl Bathurst. Under their ownership the paper became notorious by its offensive articles. In 1920 it published a series based on the Protocols of the Elders of Zion, an antisemitic hoax text previously written in Russian. These articles were later contained in a book entitled "The Cause of World Unrest", to which many of the paper's staff contributed. The book, which denounced Jews and blamed them for the world's woes, was compiled under the directorship of the paper's editor, Howell Arthur Gwynne. Four years later, with public criticism unabated, the Bathursts sold the paper to a consortium headed by the Duke of Northumberland. But by then the damage had been done. A boycott of the paper by Jewish advertisers contributed to a decline. Eventually on August 24th 1937, *The Morning Post* was sold to *The Daily Telegraph*. Ironically, the *Telegraphs* owners, Lord Camrose and Lord Kemsley, were related to powerful Jewish families.

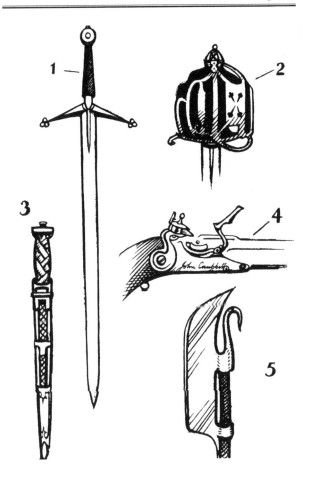

Clan weapons

1) The claymore or two-handed sword
(fifteenth or early sixteenth century)

2) Basket hilt of broadsword
made in Stirling, 1716

3) Highland dirk
(eighteenth century)

4) Steel pistol *(detail)* made in Doune

5) Head of Lochaber Axe as carried
in the '45 and earlier